Learning to Read, Step by Step!

Ready to Read   Preschool–Kindergarten
• big type and easy words • rhyme and rhythm • picture clues
For children who know the alphabet and are eager to begin reading.

Reading with Help   Preschool–Grade 1
• basic vocabulary • short sentences • simple stories
For children who recognize familiar words and sound out new words with help.

Reading on Your Own   Grades 1–3
• engaging characters • easy-to-follow plots • popular topics
For children who are ready to read on their own.

Reading Paragraphs   Grades 2–3
• challenging vocabulary • short paragraphs • exciting stories
For newly independent readers who read simple sentences with confidence.

Ready for Chapters   Grades 2–4
• chapters • longer paragraphs • full-color art
For children who want to take the plunge into chapter books but still like colorful pictures.

STEP INTO READING® is designed to give every child a successful reading experience. The grade levels are only guides; children will progress through the steps at their own speed, developing confidence in their reading. The F&P Text Level on the back cover serves as another tool to help you choose the right book for your child.

Remember, a lifetime love of reading starts with a single step!

For all those who love dogs, care for dogs, and read to dogs. And for Clover and Penny, who are very good dogs. They are! Yes, they are! —E.S.P.

To Comet —M.S.

Acknowledgments: The author and editor gratefully acknowledge the help of Jim Breheny, Director of the Bronx Zoo and Executive Vice President of the Wildlife Conservation Society Zoos & Aquarium. Thank you very much!

Text copyright © 2022 by Erica S. Perl
Cover art and interior illustrations copyright © 2022 by Michael Slack

Photograph credits: Front and back cover: Erik Lam/Dreamstime; p. 3: Tierfotoagentur/Alamy Stock Photo; p. 4: Arterra Picture Library/Alamy Stock Photo; p. 5: Jove Pargovski/Dreamstime; p. 8: Nattaphon Moontichai/Dreamstime; p. 9 (top): Zuzana Tillerová/Dreamstime; p. 9 (bottom): Sonsedskaya/Dreamstime; p. 12: Darius Strazdas/Dreamstime; p. 13: Martin Schlecht/Dreamstime; p. 16: Kim Christensen/Alamy Stock Photo; p. 17: petfoto/Alamy Stock Photo; p. 20: Alexirina27000/Dreamstime; p. 21 (top and bottom): Isselee/Dreamstime; p. 24: Allstar Picture Library Ltd/Alamy Stock Photo; p. 25 (top): Pojoslaw/Dreamstime; p 25 (bottom): Kittiphan Teerawattanakul/Dreamstime; p. 28: Redwood8/Dreamstime; p. 29 (top): Waldemar Dabrowski/Dreamstime; p. 29 (bottom) blinckwinkel/Kopp/Alamy Stock Photo; p. 32: Peter Newark American Pictures/Bridgeman Images; p. 33: National Gallery of Art/Wikimedia Commons; p. 36: Danita Delimont Creative/Alamy Stock Photo; p. 37 (top): Mikael Males/Dreamstime; p. 37 (bottom): Dssimages/Dreamstime; p. 40: Erica S. Perl; p. 41: Philippe Demande/Dreamstime; p. 44: Associated Press; p. 45: PA Images/Alamy Stock Photo

Visit us on the Web!
StepIntoReading.com
rhcbooks.com

Educators and librarians, for a variety of teaching tools, visit us at RHTeachersLibrarians.com

Library of Congress Cataloging-in-Publication Data
Names: Perl, Erica S., author. | Slack, Michael, illustrator.
Title: Truth or lie: dogs! / by Erica S. Perl; illustrations by Michael Slack.
Description: New York: Random House Children's Books, [2022] |
Identifiers: LCCN 2021021447 | ISBN 978-0-593-42910-5 (trade paperback) |
ISBN 978-0-593-42911-2 (library binding) | ISBN 978-0-593-42912-9 (ebook)
Subjects: LCSH: Dogs—Juvenile literature. | Puppies—Juvenile literature.
Classification: LCC SF426.5 .P43 2022 | DDC 636.7—dc23

Printed in the United States of America
10 9 8 7 6 5 4 3 2 1

STEP INTO READING®

TRUTH or LIE
DOGS!

by Erica S. Perl

illustrations by Michael Slack

Random House 🏠 New York

Hi! I'm the TRUTH SLEUTH.

As you can see,

I run with the big dogs.

And the small dogs, too!

Dogs have been loyal companions
for well over
eleven thousand years.
That's TRUE!
But I spy a LIE nearby.
Let's play TRUTH OR LIE
and find it!
When you turn the page,
you'll see four statements . . .
BUT only three are TRUE.

Can you find a tiny little LIE
about puppies?
Give it a try!

1. Puppies are born with
   toenails.

2. Puppies are born with teeth.

3. Puppies are born blind and deaf.

4. Puppies sleep up to twenty-two
hours a day.

The lie is #2!

Puppies are born with teeth.

Newborn puppies have fur and tails
and sharp little toenails.
But they don't have teeth yet.
And they can't see or hear.

Just give them time!
In one to two months,
most puppies will be able
to see, hear, run,
and wag their tails.

They will chew on everything
with the new puppy teeth
they've grown!

Can you sniff out another LIE?

1. Only 10 percent of dogs greet other dogs by sniffing their butts.

Hello. Want a sniff?

No thanks.

2. Dog noses are 10,000 to 100,000 times more sensitive than human noses.

VS

3. Dogs' right and left nostrils
   pick up scents separately.

4. Dog noses have a special
   chamber that holds scents
   so dogs can figure out
   what they are.

The lie is #1.

Only 10 percent of dogs greet other dogs by sniffing their butts.

For dogs, butt sniffing is like saying hello, but with added benefits. The scent made by a dog's anal glands (that's right—in its butt) gives important information to other dogs.

A good butt sniff
tells one dog
if it has already met
the other dog,
whether that dog is healthy,
and much more.
That's why almost all dogs
greet each other this way.

Can you fetch another LIE?

1. Dogs move their tails to signal many different emotions.

2. Dogs are capable of dreaming when they sleep.

3. One of the ways dogs cool down

   is by sweating

   through their paws.

4. Dogs can only see

   black and white.

The lie is #4!

Dogs can only see black and white.

Many people think dogs

can't see colors.

But it's not true.

Dogs' eyes have

two types of color receptors

(called cones).

Most people's eyes have three.

So dogs do not see all colors,

but they see more than

just black and white.

Many people also think
dogs don't sweat.
They actually have
sweat glands in their paw pads.
(This makes some dogs' feet
smell like popcorn.)

Can you point out a LIE about different dog breeds?

1. The basenji is a breed of dog that does not bark.

Is your bark broken?

2. The Peruvian Inca Orchid is a breed of dog that can be hairless.

Aren't you cold?

3. The borzoi is a breed of dog
   with a blue tongue.

4. The Norwegian lundehund
   has six toes on each foot.

The lie is #3.

The borzoi is a breed  **of dog with a blue tongue.**

The breed that is famous for having a blue tongue is the chow chow.

It's not the only breed
with an unexpected
tongue color.

Shar-pei dogs have
blue-black tongues.
There are so many
unusual kinds of dogs!
Dogs can have lots of fur
or no fur at all.

Shake.

Some have unique markings.
And many have
one-of-a-kind personalities.

You're doing a great job. Keep up the good work by finding another LIE!

1. In Telluride, Colorado, dogs rescue people from avalanches.

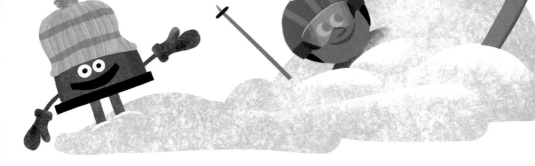

2. In Washington, DC, dogs work at Union Station, sniffing out illegal drugs.

3. In London, England,
   dogs fetch lost balls during
   Wimbledon tennis matches.

4. In Queenstown,
   New Zealand,
   dogs herd sheep and
   guard them from predators.

The lie is #3.

In London, England, dogs fetch lost balls during Wimbledon tennis matches.

At Wimbledon,
the job of retrieving
lost tennis balls
is given to kids,
not dogs (sorry, dogs!).

But dogs perform
many important jobs
all over the world.
Their excellent sense of
smell, tracking skills,
and desire to work with
people help them succeed.

Can you lead me to a LIE?

1. Service dogs assist people with disabilities.

2. Guide dogs, hearing dogs, and medical alert dogs are all types of service dogs.

3. Service dogs need to be trained.

4. The Labrador retriever is the only breed that can become a service dog.

Yeah, Sandy!

The lie is #4!

The Labrador retriever is the only breed that can become a service dog.

Many service dogs are Labrador retrievers. But this is not the only breed that can become a service dog.

For example, a papillon can make an excellent hearing dog.

And mixed-breed dogs can be trained as service dogs, too.

I need your vote! Which is a lie about presidential pups?

1. George Washington's dogs were the first canines to live at the White House.

2. When Barack Obama became president, he kept a promise to his daughters and got them a dog.

3. The Franklin Delano Roosevelt
   Memorial in Washington, DC,
   includes a larger-than-life statue
   of his Scottish terrier, Fala.

4. A German shepherd named Major,
   owned by President Joe Biden,
   became the first shelter dog
   to live at the White House.

The lie is #1.

George Washington's dogs were the first canines to live at the White House.

The father of our country loved dogs and owned many of them during his time as president.

But George Washington
never lived in the White House,
and neither did his dogs.
The White House was not finished
being built until
after Washington left office.
So John Adams's two dogs
were the first presidential pups
to relieve themselves
on the White House lawn.

Howwwwl . . . would you like
a LIE about wolves?

1. Wolves are closely related to
dogs.

2. Baby wolves are called kits.

3. Wolves live in family groups called packs.

4. A wolf's howl can be heard ten miles away.

The lie is #2.

Baby wolves are called kits.

Baby wolves are called pups.
In many ways,
wolf pups look and act
like their dog relatives.
They play with their littermates.

They drink milk
from their mothers.
And they sleep in a
big, cozy pile.

As they grow, they take
their places in the pack,
learning to hide, hunt,
and howl like adult wolves.

Can you spot a LIE
about African wild dogs?

1. African wild dogs
   hunt as a team
   to take down larger animals
   like wildebeest.

2. The scientific name for the African
   wild dog means "painted wolf."

3. African wild dogs can run over forty miles per hour.

4. African wild dogs can be found in every African country.

The lie is #4.

African wild dogs can be found in every African country.

African wild dogs are endangered. It is estimated that there are fewer than seven thousand left, and they are only found in some African countries.

Scientists and conservationists are working to support and increase wild dog populations, so that one day they might live throughout Africa again.

I've got you covered.

There's one more lie?
Now, that's incredible!

1. In 1925, teams of sled dogs
   ran a relay race across Alaska
   to deliver medicine and
   stop a deadly epidemic.

   Nome

   ALASKA

   Nenahna

2. In 1926, a tiny fox terrier
   named Titina flew by airship
   to the North Pole.

3. A German shepherd named Apollo was honored for being the only dog to help at Ground Zero after the 9/11 World Trade Center attacks.

4. In 1903, a goggle-wearing dog, Bud, joined the first car trip across America.

Come back here!

The lie is #3.

A German shepherd named Apollo was honored for being the only dog to help at Ground Zero after the 9/11 World Trade Center attacks.

On September 11, 2001, Apollo was the first search-and-rescue dog at the World Trade Center.

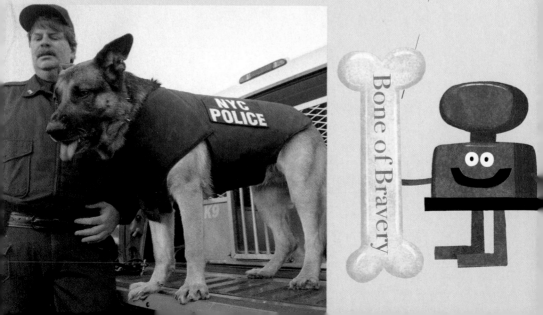

Bone of Bravery

But he was not the only one.
Apollo received
the Dickin Medal
on behalf of all the
search-and-rescue dogs
at Ground Zero
and the Pentagon!

Good dog!

Er . . . I mean . . . you did it!

You are officially a

TRUTH SLEUTH like me.

Keep up the good work!

- Read with an eye for TRUTH and a nose for LIES.

- Share what you know *and* how you figured out it was TRUE.

- Ask your parents, guardian, teacher, or librarian to help you dig up the best books and most reliable websites.

- Play TRUTH OR LIE with your friends and family.

Want to Learn More FACTS About Dogs?

Books to read:

The Best Book of Wolves and Wild Dogs by Christiane
Gunzi (Macmillan, 2003)

Dogs by Seymour Simon (HarperCollins, 2009)

The Everything Book of Dogs & Puppies by Andrea Mills
(DK, 2018)

Everything Dogs by Becky Baines (National Geographic,
2012)

Sniffer Dogs: How Dogs (and Their Noses) Save the World
by Nancy F. Castaldo (Houghton Mifflin Harcourt,
2014)

Websites to check out:

akc.org

aspca.org/pet-care

canine.org

petfinder.com/dogs/

tdi-dog.org